WASTE AND RECYCLING

Barbara James

STECK-VAUGHN
L I B R A R Y
A Division of Steck-Vaughn Company

Conserving Our World

Acid Rain
Conserving Rain Forests
Waste and Recycling
Conserving the Atmosphere
Protecting Wildlife
The Spread of Deserts

Cover: A pile of wrecked cars at a dump site.

Series editor: Sue Hadden
Series designer: Ross George

Published in the United States in 1990 by Steck-Vaughn Co., Austin, Texas, a subsidiary of National Education Corporation.

Copyright 1989 Wayland (Publishers) Ltd

First published in 1989 by
Wayland (Publishers) Ltd

Library of Congress Cataloging-in-Publication Data

James, Barbara, 1953-
    Waste and recycling / Barbara James.
      p. cm. — (Conserving our world)
    ''First published in 1989 by Wayland (Publishers) Ltd.—
T.p. verso
    Includes bibliographical references.
    Summary: Discusses types of waste, including domestic, industrial, agricultural, and radioactive, and how it can be handled and controlled.
    ISBN 0-8114-3457-5 Softcover Binding
    ISBN 0-8114-2386-7 Hardcover Library Binding
    1. Refuse and refuse disposal—Juvenile literature.
2. Recycling (Waste, etc.)—Juvenile literature. [1. Refuse and refuse disposal.] I. Title. II. Series.
TD792.J35 1990
363.72'8—dc20   89-26274
                         CIP
                         AC

Typeset by Multifacit Graphics, Keyport, NJ
Printed in the United States.
Bound in the United States by Lake Book, Melrose Park, IL

5 6 7 8 9 0 LB 94 93 92

Contents

The voyage of the *Karin B*

In late August 1988 the *Karin B*, a West German freighter, was anchored off the Cornish coast of Great Britain. A Royal Navy vessel was standing guard. The captain of the *Karin B* was hoping to end his two-month voyage around the seas looking for a port that would let his ship dock—with its cargo. The *Karin B* had already been refused entry in Italy, Germany, and Spain because it was carrying 167 containers holding more than 2,000 tons of poisonous waste chemicals.

This toxic waste itself was well traveled. It is

In August 1988 the Karin B toured European ports in search of one that would accept its cargo of toxic waste. Eventually, it was forced to return to Italy, where it had started its long journey.

uncertain where it was originally produced but it was dumped illegally in Nigeria by an Italian company. When Nigeria ordered its removal, the *Karin B* was hired to pick up the deadly cargo and return it to Italy. However, the Italian authorities refused entry to their ports and so began the voyage of the *Karin B*.

In Britain, the government was under intense pressure from the public and the press to stop the ship from entering Plymouth harbor. Permission to dock was refused and the *Karin B* set off again. The captain, Richard Hinterleitner said, ''I don't think I'll be handling toxic waste again.''

The *Karin B's* voyage is short compared to those of the barges *Khian Sea* and *Bark*. They have been at sea for eighteen months looking for somewhere to dump their cargoes of stinking sewage. They have sailed from the United States, where the sewage originated, to the Caribbean in their search for a port that will accept them.

These three ships and many more are carrying the waste that nobody wants. Not all waste is so difficult to dispose of, or so deadly, but the disposal of waste is a ''hot'' environmental issue

because of the way it can affect our planet. In this book we shall look at the different types of waste, how they are dealt with, and the effects that waste can have on the Earth's natural cycles. The waste story is not without solutions—refuse, reclamation, and recycling are vital alternative methods of handling waste and this book will look at some plans in operation. It will also give you some ideas about what you can do to reduce reuse, and recycle waste.

Greenpeace, an environmental pressure group, aims to influence public and political opinion by nonviolent campaigning. It has publicized environmental issues, such as the pollution of the North Sea from sewage and waste.

What is Waste?

Nature and waste

What happens to wild birds and animals when they die? Where do all the leaves go once they have fallen in autumn? They are dealt with by nature's recycling system. All dead plants and animals decay and decompose. They are broken down by maggots, worms, bacteria, and fungi and so the chemicals and nutrients they contain return to the earth. They may go into the soil, the ocean, or perhaps a river, where they are used again by growing plants and animals. This is a natural process in which waste materials are reused. It is a never-ending cycle of death, decay, new life, and growth.

A good example of this cycle is a garden compost heap. Compost heaps are valuable because they rot down garden waste, as well as vegetable peelings and waste food, and produce humus. Humus is dug back into the soil where it aids new growth and improves the structure and texture of the soil.

Nature is very efficient at dealing with waste. In fact, it is not really waste because it is used again and becomes a resource. A dead tree trunk

The diagram below shows a woodland recycling system. All healthy habitats have such cycles but when they become polluted, the cycles are in danger of breaking down.

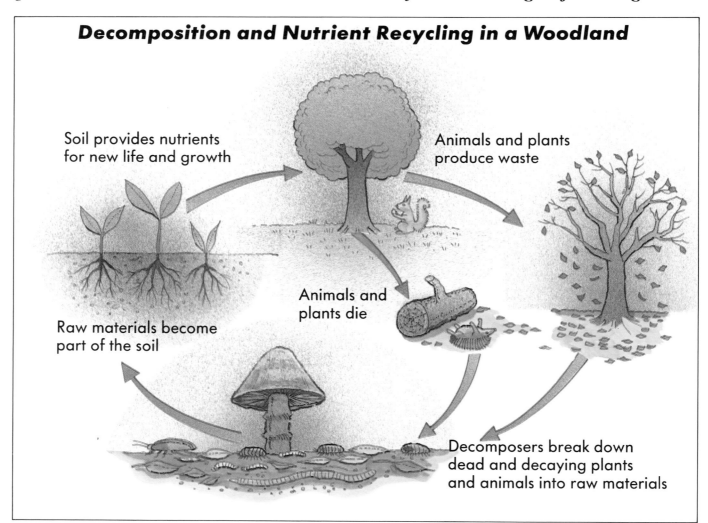

Decomposition and Nutrient Recycling in a Woodland

Soil provides nutrients for new life and growth

Animals and plants produce waste

Animals and plants die

Raw materials become part of the soil

Decomposers break down dead and decaying plants and animals into raw materials

A mountain of unwanted cars. Unlike many consumer products, cars are usually recycled for their scrap metal.

A dead tree trunk is a valuable resource for the pileated woodpecker, which is using it for a nest hole.

becomes a home for insects and birds, such as woodpeckers, before it eventually rots down into the earth to become humus. On the rocks of the west coast of South America are huge colonies of fish-eating birds. Their droppings are rich in the mineral phosphorous, that helps plants to grow. These enormous deposits of bird droppings, or "guano," have been used as an agricultural fertilizer by humans. So what is waste to one species is a resource to another.

While nature is very good at reuse and recycling, humans can be very efficient at wasting materials. In one day the United States disposes of 90 million bottles and jars; 46 million cans; and 25,000 television sets. Although some of these resources are used again, most of them are dumped as garbage. As more and more accumulates, the demand for holes in the ground, landfill sites, in which to deposit waste has grown rapidly. Human waste may travel many miles before it is finally dumped—domestic waste from New York is transported to landfill sites in neighboring states as well as out to sea.

Many waste products do not decompose easily. Here in Manitoba, Canada, polar bears forage for food in a garbage dump.

The Earth's natural cycles of decomposition and recycling can cope with some human waste. However the huge amount of waste that humans throw away is overloading the system. The problem is made worse because many of the substances manufactured by humans are not biodegradable. This means that they do not decompose easily. Glass, tin, and some plastics are not biodegradable and they take many years to break down. Waste materials that are dumped and do not decompose quickly may cause pollution.

Pollution

When humans are wasteful with the Earth's resources and do not reuse or recycle materials, the environment becomes polluted with waste products. Pollution prevents the Earth's natural cycles from working properly. It is also unsightly and often dangerous.

Polluted environments are a health hazard — they threaten the health of our planet, as well as our own lives. If domestic waste is not taken away from our homes, there would soon be mounds of rotting waste that would attract flies and rats. Although these animals perform a useful function in helping to decompose waste, they can also carry disease that is deadly to humans. Similarly, if factories are allowed to continue to pour chemical waste into rivers and oceans, the planet's water will become poisoned.

The Unique Planet

The Earth is the only planet known to support life. It has all the resources and materials to enable plants and animals, including humans, to survive. The Earth provides water, air, energy, food, minerals, metals, and medicines, as well as recycling systems so that the resources are reused. It also supports our quality of life—arts,

sciences, recreation, and religious beliefs.

These resources and materials, however, are limited and need to be used wisely and conserved. The Earth's natural systems are vital to life but they will break down if they are overloaded. The survival and well-being of life on Earth is linked to the environment. Our own lives and those of future generations depend on us treating the Earth with care and respect.

Domestic Waste

The consumer society

We live in a society that consumes, or uses, many resources. It is often called "the consumer society" and this usually refers to Western countries including the United States and Canada, Europe, Japan, Australia, and New Zealand. These countries have developed lifestyles that use many products such as cars, televisions, furniture, refrigerators, books, and cosmetics. Lifestyles like these consume many of the world's resources.

These societies have not always used so much. During World War II, materials and resources were scarce because trading systems did not, or could not, operate. Countries had to introduce rationing of food and other necessities such as gasoline, and people were encouraged to conserve and recycle materials. For example, women reused old dresses to make new ones.

Many of the world's resources are used to enable the consumer society to have labor-saving devices. How many kitchen gadgets do you use in your home?

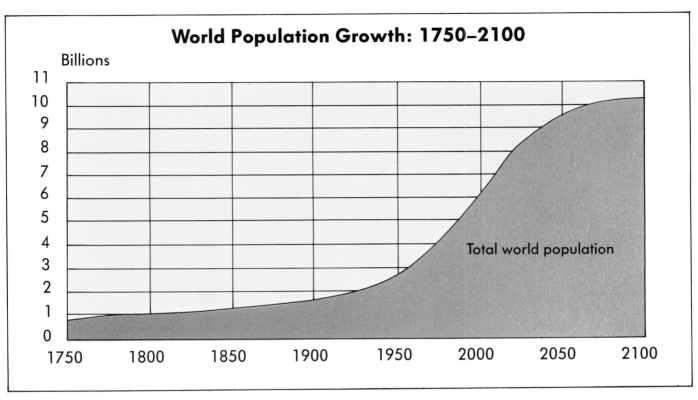

World Population Growth: 1750–2100

Billions

Total world population

1750   1800   1850   1900   1950   2000   2050   2100

The above graph shows the rise in the world's population since 1750 and the predicted population for 2000 and 2100.

Right *One-third of the world's population uses over 85% of the world's resources. The other 15% is used by the rest of the world.*

In the years since World War II, the world population has increased dramatically. Cities have become larger because, throughout the world, there is a trend toward urbanization. This means that people leave rural communities to seek a living in the city. City-dwellers, particularly in Western countries, require food and goods to be brought into the city. They wish to have convenience foods and luxury items, such as freezers and videocassette players. They use and throw away large amounts of materials, especially packaging. In a city environment, natural recycling systems cannot operate. There is too much waste for them to cope with.

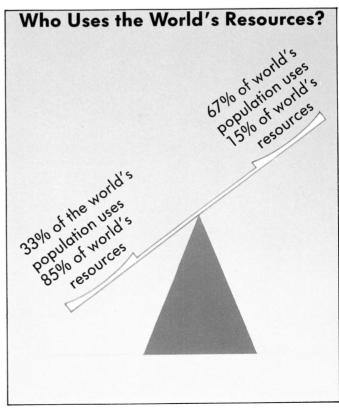

Who Uses the World's Resources?

67% of world's population uses 15% of world's resources

33% of the world's population uses 85% of world's resources

Throwing it away

Look at what *you* throw away each day. Soda cans, candy wrappers, leftover food, paper, and bottles are just some of the items to be found in a typical garbage can. You may think this is all garbage but they are valuable resources—paper, glass, plastic, metal.

Much of the contents of a garbage can is packaging. The cardboard, paper, and plastic containers surrounding a product are designed to make it more attractive to the buyer, but all this

In many countries, people make their living by reusing other people's waste. The photograph shows a waste site in the Philippines.

You can see from the illustration below *the packaging for a few chocolates.*

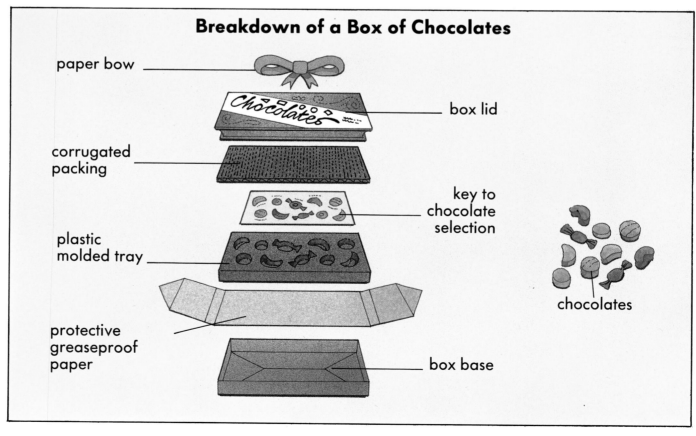

Breakdown of a Box of Chocolates

paper bow

box lid

corrugated packing

key to chocolate selection

plastic molded tray

protective greaseproof paper

box base

chocolates

One Person's Waste Each Year

5 lbs. of aluminum cans

about 10 times his/her own body weight in household garbage

2 trees worth of paper

72 lbs. of tin cans

80 lbs. of glass bottles and jars

88 lbs. of plastics

SOURCE: Franklin Associates, Ltd., 1988

The above diagram illustrates the average amount of waste produced by one person in one year.

packaging is thrown away. Paper and cardboard form two-thirds of the waste from homes.

The packaging story is not all bad news, however. Some packaging is necessary to keep products such as food clean and free from contamination. Also, more and more packages are being made from recycled materials. For example, cardboard is made from recycled paper.

Waste management

Because there is so much domestic waste, we have had to devise ways to dispose of it. In Europe each household fills, on average, two garbage cans a week. Multiply this by the number of households in an entire country and you have a huge amount of waste to be dealt with. New York City throws out the most waste per person per day—approximately 4 lbs. per person. Every day New York has to dispose of about 26,000 tons of waste.

So what happens to the waste we put into our garbage cans? First it is collected, by the sanitation department or a private company, and taken to a garbage dump along with waste from the other homes in the area. At the dump some sorting of the waste may be done—scrap metal is often taken out to be melted down and reused. What happens to the waste then varies from place to place. In general, the most popular solution to the waste mountain is to bury it in landfill sites. Great Britain disposes of about 90 percent of its waste in this way.

There are problems with landfill sites, however. The decaying waste produces gases (mainly methane) that seep up through the ground. Occasionally, these gases have caused explosions

Collection of domestic waste is vital to the health of the community. Refuse collectors (insert photograph) *take the waste to a garbage dump, like this one in Japan.*

or required buildings erected on the site to be evacuated. The buried waste can also pollute the groundwater. This runs into rivers and streams that supply our drinking water.

Another method of disposal is incineration, or burning the waste. This method is becoming more popular as landfill sites are becoming scarce and, therefore, more expensive. An advantage of incineration is that energy can be produced from the burning waste, and there are now some ''energy from waste'' programs in operation. This is particularly popular in Denmark, where 75 percent of the waste is burned to produce energy. There are also drawbacks to this system of disposal. It costs a great deal of money to develop incineration systems. More seriously, the gases emitted during the burning process pollute the air.

Waste is expensive—it costs time, energy, and space, as well as money. Great Britain pays $1.6 million a day to dispose of waste into landfill sites. It is estimated that California will have to pay $1 billion a year by the 1990s to dispose of its waste. Not only does waste cost a lot of money, it can also pollute the environment. However, garbage does not need to be wasted. It can be *reused* and *recycled.*

Another method of waste disposal is incineration, or burning. Energy can be produced as a by-product but air pollution can be a problem.

Reuse and recycling

We can see examples of reuse and recycling all around us. The clothing, toys, and books passed on to friends, relatives, or thrift shops are being reused. In many areas local government, or sometimes voluntary groups, have set up recycling facilities such as bottle banks, aluminum can banks, or waste paper collections, where local people can take their recyclable garbage. City authorities are looking more and more at recycling systems because this form of waste management saves money, resources, and energy.

Recycling can also be less damaging to the environment. Paper recycling not only saves the trees that are felled to make paper, but it also reduces air and water pollution and conserves valuable energy.

Bottle banks are becoming a common feature of city life. You can help the environment by saving your glass bottles and taking them to be recycled.

16

The Oregon Example

The state of Oregon shows what can be done if there is political and popular support. Oregon has a law, the Recycling Opportunity Act, to make recycling available to all its citizens. The act aims to:

- reduce the amount of waste generated
- reuse materials where possible
- recycle non-reusable materials
- use waste that cannot be reused or recycled in "energy from waste" plans
- dispose of the remaining waste by landfilling or other appropriate methods

Oregon doesn't stop there. It also reduces the taxes paid by businesses involved in recycling systems.

Above *and* below *Centers in London and Grenoble, France, sort and separate waste for recycling. Paper, metal, and glass can be easily dealt with, but there has been little progress in processes to recycle plastics.*

Domestic waste is only a small part of the total waste produced. Industry is also responsible for large amounts of waste—coal mining dumps, slag heaps, chemical waste, and the gas and smoke that pour out of factory chimneys.

Industrialized societies need industry to produce the energy and goods that their populations expect to maintain their lifestyle. Industries include food processing, mining, petro-chemical and plastic production, metals and chemicals, paper and pulp, and the manufacture of consumer goods like televisions. In turn, industry depends on the raw materials such as iron, water, and wood to manufacture goods. This manufacturing process produces waste products and, while some of these industrial wastes are relatively harmless, others are highly toxic. The toxic wastes can do great harm to nature and to humans, particularly when they are produced in such large quantities.

The tall chimneys of power stations emit sulfur dioxide, which can drift over crops.

Hazardous waste

About 10 to 20 percent of industrial waste could be dangerous to humans and to natural systems. Hazardous waste includes chemicals like cyanide, pesticides such as DDT, solvents, asbestos, and metals such as mercury and cadmium. Industry disposes of this dangerous waste in a variety of ways. Some waste, particularly solid waste, is dumped in landfill sites, while liquid waste is often pumped into rivers or the ocean. Ninety percent of waste ends up in the ocean one way or another.

Some hazardous wastes are dumped into the environment precisely because they are so dangerous. It is not known how to deal with them safely and it is hoped that the environment can absorb the toxic substances. However, this is not a safe solution to the problem. Many metals and chemicals are not natural and are not biodegradable. Therefore, as more and more waste is dumped, the Earth's natural cycles are threatened and the environment becomes polluted. Since the 1950s chemical and toxic waste pollution disasters have become more common and more serious.

A photograph taken by Greenpeace campaigners. It shows toxic waste called yellow sludge being dumped off the coast of northern France. Every day, a French chemical company dumps 2,200 tons of this yellow sludge into the English Channel.

Waste Disasters

1959	Minimata, Japan	Mercury is discharged into waterways: 400 dead: 2,000 injured.
1974	Flixborough, UK	An explosion at a chemical plant: 23 dead; 104 injured; 3,000 evacuated.
1976	Seveso, Italy	Leakage of dioxin: 193 injured; 730 evacuated.
1978	Manfredonia, Italy	Ammonia is released from chemical plant: 10,000 evacuated.
1984	Bhopal, India	Leakage of pesticide from factory: 2,500 dead; thousands injured; 200,000 evacuated.

(Information from UNEP)

At present there are more than seven million known chemicals, and thousands of new ones are discovered every year. As more chemicals are discovered, it becomes even more difficult to deal with the waste effectively.

Pollution knows no frontiers

Hazardous waste may be produced in one country, but when it is pumped into a river, the ocean, or the atmosphere, the effects are felt in another country. In 1986, a fire at a chemical factory by the Rhine River in Switzerland resulted in serious river pollution in Germany, France, and Holland, which badly affected the North Sea. Wastes from power stations in Great Britain cause air pollution which falls as acid rain in Norway and Sweden.

Farther away, toxic substances are being found in the deep ocean trenches some distance from human settlements. Antarctica, often called "the last wilderness," has also been found to contain pollutants. The pollution has traveled across the globe from industrial nations.

Some industrial waste is so toxic that protective clothing and special equipment is needed to deal with it.

Left *In 1976 the chemical dioxin leaked from a factory in Seveso, Italy. Crops and livestock were poisoned, while many local people suffered long-term health problems.*

Below *One of the world's worst chemical disasters was at Bhopal, India, in 1984. Thousands of people were killed or injured and 200,000 people were evacuated from their homes.*

The oceans

The threat to the world's seas and oceans from waste and pollution is becoming obvious. The North Sea has long been a dumping ground for waste from many European countries. Chemicals such as PCBs (polychlorinated biphenols), and pesticides such as DDT, as well as domestic waste, oil, incinerated waste, and sewage are all regularly disposed of at sea. The ocean is used as a sewer and there will have to be an international effort to clean it up.

Above *Oil pollution is a serious threat to the world's oceans and has a devastating effect on coastline habitats. This oil spill occurred in San Francisco Bay.*

Left *Pollution of the North Sea is widely thought to have contributed to the death of many gray seals during 1988.*

The Beluga Whale – Victim of Toxic Waste

In Canada, stocks of the white Beluga whale in the St. Lawrence Seaway are severely reduced. In 1900, 5,000 whales lived in the seaway and now there are estimated to be 450 whales. Researchers believe that toxic waste from industrial sites along the river is causing the whales to die from blood poisoning. Examinations of their bodies have shown a very high level of harmful chemicals, including PCBs, DDT, mercury, and cadmium.

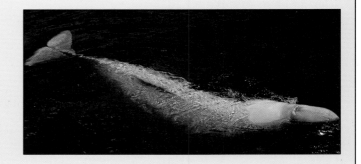

The beautiful beluga, or white whale, is probably earth's most polluted mammal.

An end to the dumping?

The toxic waste situation has become more serious with disasters occurring more frequently. At last humans have been made aware of what they are doing to their planet. Environmental pressure groups such as Greenpeace and Friends of the Earth have campaigned to bring this pollution to the attention of governments and the public. As public awareness and press attention has grown, there have been moves to restrict the dumping of waste. Some regulations have been tightened but it is a slow process and alternative disposal methods have to be found.

Importing and Exporting Pollution

Great Britain has been called "the garbage dump of Europe" because it imports toxic wastes from other countries. Holland, Ireland, Belgium, the United States, Canada, and many other countries pay Great Britain to dispose of their waste. Most of this waste is put into landfill sites but some is incinerated or treated. The United Kingdom Royal Commission on Environmental Pollution has expressed its concern over the trade in waste into Britain. It has called for improved regulations on hazardous waste treatment and disposal.

Greenpeace campaigners often attempt to stop the dumping of waste into the ocean. The photograph, taken in 1982, shows six members of Greenpeace chaining themselves to a ship dumping waste in the Atlantic. Such protests are often effective.

As antipollution laws have become stricter in developed countries, industries have looked elsewhere to dispose of their waste. Many developing countries in the Third World have become dump sites for industrial waste. A report by Greenpeace shows that waste from Europe and the United States is dumped unmonitored in many countries of Africa and South America. The United Nations Environment Program is now working to reduce the widespread international trade in toxic waste.

Agricultural Waste

More than two billion tons of manure is produced each year by livestock in the United States. This large amount of waste is the result of changes in farming practices during the last thirty years. It also has produced extensive research into the ways that all this waste can be utilized. Before 1960, American farmers raised livestock in fields, and depended on crop rotations to keep the soil healthy. Over the years, farming has become more specialized and intensive. More animals are raised in smaller areas, and often indoors. Farmers can produce more food this way but the animals need more care. Their feed has to be taken to them and their waste has to be taken away. Farmers today use large amounts of pesticides and fertilizers to make crops grow rapidly and produce large harvests. While this is economically efficient, it also creates surpluses and waste.

Intensive farming involves keeping many animals in a small area, as on this farm in Australia.

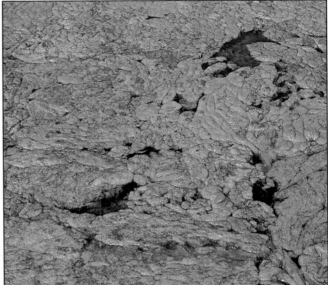

Main picture *Intensively farmed animals produce much waste, which is stored in slurry lagoons or pits. Often it leaks into the ground, polluting the groundwater. The* inset *photograph shows the build up of algae when fertilizers are washed into rivers and ponds. The nitrates they contain prevent oxygen from reaching other creatures.*

Animal Waste

Intensive livestock production involves raising more animals in a smaller area, which in turn means more manure. Some large U.S. feedlots have more than 100,000 head of cattle in pens at any one time. The massive amounts of manure these cattle produce cannot be recycled naturally, so systems have been developed to store and dispose of it. At the farm, the waste, or slurry, is kept in pits and later spread onto the fields. If it is spread too thickly the natural cycles of decomposition cannot operate. This causes some

of the waste to wash off into the groundwater or into rivers and streams, causing water pollution. The pits may also leak waste into these water courses. Pollution of rivers and streams is increasing and many incidents are linked to agricultural practices.

The pollution of rivers and streams by organic waste can threaten the life cycles in the water. Waste entering the water is gradually broken down by microorganisms, but these use up much oxygen when dealing with the pollutants. This can result in not enough oxygen being left for other life, such as fish and plants.

Fertilizers

Modern arable farmers use chemical fertilizers containing nitrogen to improve plant growth and increase food production. All plants need minerals such as potassium, nitrogen, and phosphorus for growth. A healthy soil can provide these but artificial fertilizers add more. The nitrogen in the fertilizer is broken down by the soil to produce nitrates which are taken up by plants. Too much fertilizer produces too many nitrates and some are not absorbed by plants. Instead they are washed by rain from the soil into the groundwater or into rivers. Again, the waters are polluted, but this time by nitrates.

Water in rivers and streams is used to supply drinking water and there is now concern over the high levels of nitrates in tap water. Pollution of water supplies by nitrates is thought to be linked to various illnesses including stomach cancer and "blue baby syndrome." In 1983, an infant in Nebraska died of blue baby syndrome when commercial fertilizers caused nitrates to concentrate in groundwater. The United States is in the process of developing a national ground-water program to improve the drinking water.

The diagram shows the water cycle and also shows how organic waste and fertilizers pollute the water.

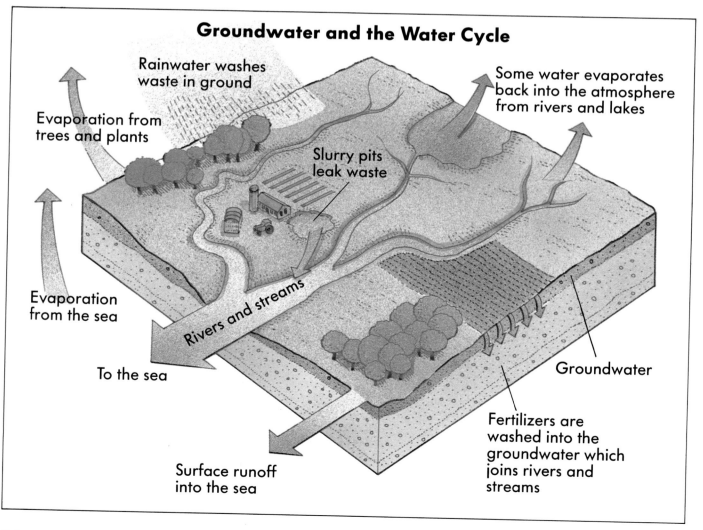

Groundwater and the Water Cycle

Rainwater washes waste in ground

Some water evaporates back into the atmosphere from rivers and lakes

Evaporation from trees and plants

Slurry pits leak waste

Evaporation from the sea

Rivers and streams

To the sea

Surface runoff into the sea

Groundwater

Fertilizers are washed into the groundwater which joins rivers and streams

Surpluses and Prices

In order to keep farm prices high, and more farmers in business, the U.S. Government buys surplus milk, grain, and meat. Without these purchases, thousands of farmers would go out of business, making food prices go up even more.

The Government gives, or sells at reduced prices, tons of farm products to food banks or schools every year. In 1984, for example, the Government gave away ten million pounds of cheese per month.

Occasionally, this food "goes bad" in storage before it is distributed. In those cases, it could be sold for animal feed, used by industries, or further processed into other food products. U.S. farmers are among the most productive in the world.

The U.S. Government buys millions of pounds of food for school lunch programs, thus using up some surplus.

Each farmer produces enough wheat for himself and 70 other people around the world.

Radioactive Waste

What is radioactivity?

In 1896, a French scientist, Antoine-Heuri Becquerel, was studying the element uranium. By chance, he placed the uranium close to a photographic plate and, when looking at the plate some time later, he saw unusual dark marks upon it. The uranium was giving out, or emitting, particles (or "rays") that were affecting the plate. This was the discovery of radiation.

Radiation is emitted by many other elements as well as uranium—radium, potassium, thorium, carbon, and iodine are just a few. These elements are said to be radioactive. All radiation can be harmful to humans and other animals because it can damage living cells. The greater the amount of radiation, the greater the possibility of damage. People have used this characteristic of radiation to treat some illnesses, such as cancer. A certain dose of radiation is given to the patient to kill cancerous body cells.

Radioactive materials are used in agriculture, industry, medicine, scientific research, and engineering, as well as in the production of nuclear power and nuclear weapons. All these processes produce wastes that are radioactive and have to be disposed of. Although all radioactivity decays (or fades) with time, it takes some radioactive materials many millions of years to do so. It is important, therefore, that waste is stored safely if it is not to harm the present and future generations of life on Earth.

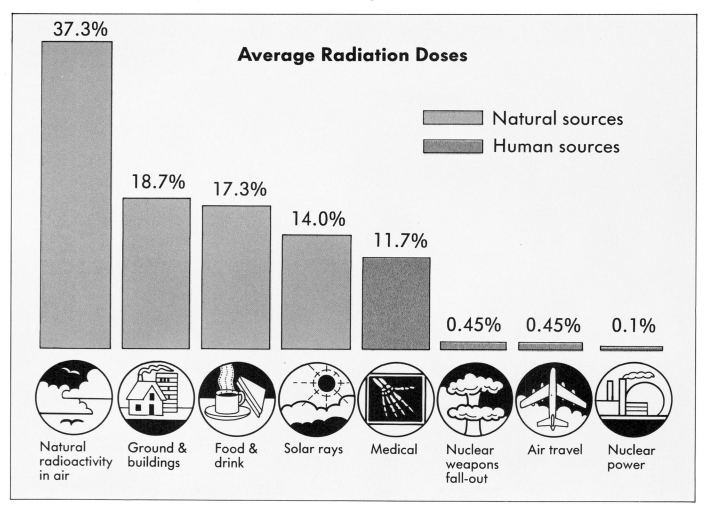

Average Radiation Doses

Natural sources / Human sources

37.3% Natural radioactivity in air · 18.7% Ground & buildings · 17.3% Food & drink · 14.0% Solar rays · 11.7% Medical · 0.45% Nuclear weapons fall-out · 0.45% Air travel · 0.1% Nuclear power

28

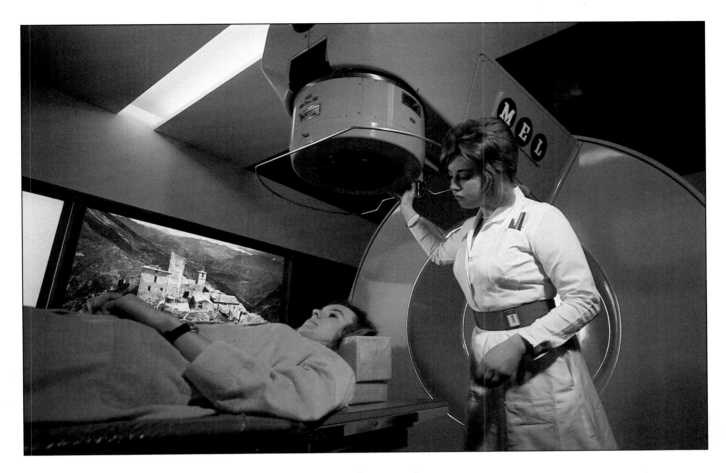

Above *Radiation can be used to treat many forms of cancer.*

The diagram opposite illustrates average radiation doses from natural and human sources. You can see that natural radioactivity in the air accounts for most of it.

Low-level waste

This is short-lived waste that has a low radioactive content. It includes contaminated protective clothing and some equipment from hospitals, factories, universities, and from the nuclear power industry.

Disposal methods include burial in trenches in the ground, dumping at sea in steel drums (this is no longer allowed in some countries); some liquid wastes are pumped into the ocean, and waste gases are discharged into the atmosphere.

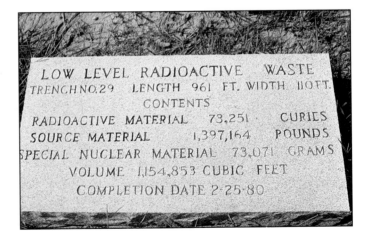

LOW LEVEL RADIOACTIVE WASTE
TRENCH NO. 29   LENGTH 961 FT. WIDTH 110 FT.
CONTENTS
RADIOACTIVE MATERIAL   73,251   CURIES
SOURCE MATERIAL   1,397,164   POUNDS
SPECIAL NUCLEAR MATERIAL   73,071   GRAMS
VOLUME 1,154,853 CUBIC FEET
COMPLETION DATE 2-25-80

Low-level radioactive waste is often buried in the ground. This marker provides some information about the type and amount of waste buried at a site in the United States.

Intermediate-level waste

This list includes bulkier solid wastes such as used equipment, transportation flasks, and radioactive sludges from power stations, fuel reprocessing plants, and nuclear weapons establishments.

Disposal methods include encasing in concrete and storing at special sites, usually at nuclear power stations. Researchers are looking into methods of disposal in deep underground sites or underneath the seabed.

High-level waste

Highly radioactive waste consists of used fuel rods and liquid waste from the nuclear power industry. It has to be kept cool.

Disposal methods include the following: liquids are stored in stainless steel tanks surrounded by concrete at special sites; they can also be solidified in glass and stored in steel containers in concrete vaults or deep underground. Researchers are also looking at ocean-bed disposal.

Above *In October 1988 German Greenpeace campaigners protested against the dumping of Swedish nuclear waste in their country. Greenpeace members have also successfully stopped the dumping of radioactive waste in the Atlantic Ocean.*

Opposite *These drums of radioactive waste are being transported to a special disposal site. Strict security and safety measures are necessary, including encasing the waste in concrete and steel.*

How to dispose of radioactive wastes safely is a controversial issue. Many people are worried by radioactivity, especially since it cannot be seen, touched, smelled, or tasted. A large number of local groups have campaigned against the disposal of waste in their area. Environmental pressure groups have also undertaken long campaigns to stop the dumping of radioactive waste. In 1983 a successful Greenpeace campaign led to the end of dumping in the Atlantic. In 1984 Greenpeace campaigners temporarily blocked the pipes pumping liquid radioactive waste from the British Sellafield nuclear plant into the Irish Sea.

Nuclear Power and Radioactivity—The Risks

Large amounts of electrical energy are needed to light and heat houses, cook food, travel, and provide power for industry. In developed countries, electricity is readily available in most homes, offices, and factories and it is generated at power stations using coal, oil, nuclear energy.

All energy production produces waste and involves risks to humans and the environment. Coal-mining waste is piled up into heaps; there are pit disasters that kill miners; and the coal power stations' waste gases contribute to the acid rain problem. Oil rigs burn off waste gas and oil, and oil-exploration disasters, like the Piper Alpha explosion in 1988, can occur.

While an adequate supply of electrical power is essential to the modern world, the various types of energy must be carefully examined. Above all, the risks to human and environmental health have to be taken into account.

In July 1988, an explosion at the Piper Alpha oil rig in the North Sea killed 167 people.

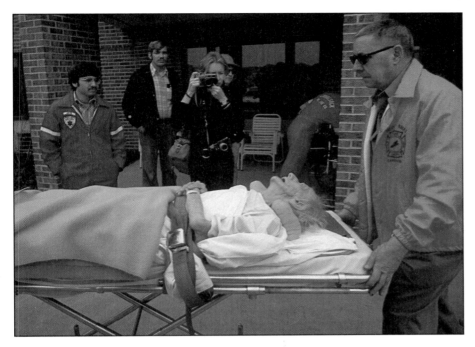

The nuclear accident at Three Mile Island, in 1979, resulted in the evacuation of many people from their homes.

Nuclear power is an important source of energy but its waste products are dangerous. Apart from the problem of radioactive waste, there have been several major nuclear accidents. In 1957, a fire at Windscale in Great Britain resulted in radioactive contamination of surrounding farmland. In 1979 at Three Mile Island, Pennsylvania, an accident in the nuclear reactor contaminated the site and cost $1 billion to clean up.

The most serious nuclear accident occurred at the Chernobyl power station in the Soviet Union in 1986. An explosion and fire sent radioactive materials into the surrounding area, which caused the evacuation of towns and villages. The area is highly radioactive and will remain so for many years. The radioactive particles, called "fall-out," were carried by winds to other countries, including Sweden, Germany, and Great Britain. Even several years later, land and grass in some areas of Britain are still radioactive, with the result that sheep grazing there become radioactive and are unfit to be eaten by humans. Worst affected of all were the reindeer herds and the Lapp people in northern Sweden. The animals and some herders are still highly radioactive.

In the Soviet Union strawberries are tested for radiation, after the 1986 explosion at the Chernobyl nuclear power station.

Further Sources of Waste

Sewage

What goes down the sink, the drain, and the toilet is called sewage and it is one of the biggest sources of waste. In most areas, to protect public health, sewage is collected in sewers and drains leading to a sewage treatment plant. The wastes are separated here, with the liquids being cleaned and returned to the river. The solids are processed to form "sludge" which is disposed of on the land or in the sea. The gases given off by the sewage can be used to produce electricity to run the treatment plant.

Many towns, however, still pour untreated sewage into rivers or the ocean. At the coastline, beaches and the water can become so seriously polluted that swimming is unsafe because of the health risks. If it is unhealthy for humans, it must harm the plants and animals even more.

Above *Marine life can be poisoned by the wastes dumped at sea. The lumps on this fish are probably caused by toxic waste.*

Below *This San Francisco beach was closed because of the high levels of sewage waste.*

Medical waste

Hospitals and clinics have waste products to be disposed of which may be infectious or contaminated. They also must dispose of waste drugs and medicines that could be harmful to the wrong person. In addition, hospitals produce a large amount of ordinary waste and this is disposed of in the same way as normal domestic waste. Contaminated hospital waste is usually incinerated on the site but in 1988 beaches in New York and New Jersey were closed after the discovery of dangerous hospital waste washed up on them. The New York City Health Department

A beach at Coney Island, in Brooklyn, lies deserted. Dangerous medical waste, including infected syringes, has been washed up on such beaches, after being illegally dumped in the ocean.

suspects that the waste was dumped in the sea illegally, but the incident highlights the problem of unlawful dumping and the need to dispose of contaminated waste safely.

If you have waste drugs or medicines at home, you should not burn them or throw or flush them away. They should be returned to the chemist or pharmacist, who can dispose of them safely.

Vehicle exhausts

Above *Exhaust fumes from vehicles are harmful to humans and the environment.*

Below *This man's car was converted to run on methane gas produced from manure.*

The waste gases from cars also pollute the environment and can harm people's health. Vehicle exhaust pipes are responsible for producing most of the carbon monoxide and lead in the air, as well as being a major contributor to the acid rain problem. Lead is highly toxic and can be very damaging to children and unborn babies. To create a safer environment, lead-free gasoline is now being promoted in many nations. Exhaust gases also contain hydrocarbons and nitrogen oxides which contribute to smog, a form of air pollution. The well-known Los Angeles smogs are largely due to car exhaust fumes.

Catalytic converters are being increasingly used to control exhaust gases. When fitted to a car, they convert the harmful gases into water vapor and carbon dioxide, but they can only be used with unleaded gasoline. Another potential solution to vehicle exhaust pollution is the "lean-burn" engine, being developed by vehicle

By using public transportation such as buses or trains, we can reduce the stress on the environment from vehicle exhaust fumes. These articulated Canadian buses can carry many passengers.

manufacturers. Such engines burn fuel more efficiently, reducing waste and pollution.

Another way of reducing waste and pollution from vehicles is to use them less frequently. If you look at the morning traffic jam into a city, you will see many cars with only one person sitting in them. Each car is using valuable energy and producing unpleasant waste. Using bicycles, buses, trains, or sharing cars are easy ways of helping the environment.

Litter

An everyday form of waste is litter. Litter is not just the candy wrappers, bus tickets, and soda cans that are thrown away, but also includes old cars that have been dumped, bottles, discarded fishing tackle, and plastic bags. Litter is any waste that has not been disposed of properly. It is another form of pollution.

Litter is found on city streets, in country lanes, and on beaches. It is usually unpleasant and ugly. It can also be dangerous—cigarette butts can cause fires, bottles can be death-traps for small mammals such as mice, and plastic bags can choke grazing animals.

Think about what you throw away. How do you feel about litter in your local area?

A small bird is freed after being entangled in fishing line thrown away by an angler.

Cleaning Up

"The best thing that can be said about the state of the world environment today is that people all over the world have started to worry about it" (United Nations Environment Program News).

The statement in this report from the United Nations Environment Program may seem gloomy, but it is a sign that changes are under way.

Humans have begun to realize how they have threatened "Mother Earth" by the careless use of her resources, by pollution, and by a disregard for her delicate natural cycles. They have also begun to see that their own health and enjoyment of life depends on a healthy environment, and that good environmental practices save money in the long run. There is still much work to be done to restore the Earth's natural balance, but there are some encouraging developments resulting from people and governments taking action.

Some children taking part in a voluntary program to clean and restore an overgrown, polluted lake. The lake had to be cleared, drained, and lined with new clay. Such restored lakes gradually become repopulated with water plants and animals.

Pressure groups and public opinion

As the state of the world environment has worsened, pressure groups have set up and campaigned to bring the situation to the attention of the public and of governments. There are now many pressure groups worldwide that are working to improve the environment. They are not just working to reduce levels of waste and pollution, but are also involved in protecting endangered wildlife and habitats, conserving energy, and improving city life, transportation, and education. This is called the Green Movement and it is growing rapidly.

There has been an "information explosion" on environmental issues. Accurate and up-to-date

As environmental issues have hit the headlines more frequently, the Green Movement has become increasingly popular, especially in West Germany and the Netherlands. Pictured above is Petra Kelly, leader of the German political party.

information is essential to monitor the state of the world and to educate and inform people. Environmental information is becoming more widely available through books, magazines, newspapers, and radio and television programs. Now an increasing number of interested and concerned people are joining together, in everything from local meetings to international conferences, to discuss environmental problems.

In Britain, government plans to establish new dumps for radioactive waste were abandoned after local people mounted campaigns to protect their environment.

Public opinion can affect environmental issues. It can generate support for particular concerns and put political pressure on local and national governments. Many surveys have been carried out on people's attitudes to the environment. A major survey carried out between 1981 and 1984 in the U.S., Japan, and Europe indicated strong public support for environmental improvement. Oil spills, air and water pollution, and nuclear and industrial waste disposal were areas of great concern.

Politics and legislation

Politicians and governments are becoming aware of public opinion on environmental issues and of the threat to the world environment. Many countries now have pollution control laws and programs to encourage waste recycling.

In 1987 The European Economic Community Environment Commission approved a five-year action plan that includes environmental protection in all economic and social policies. The following year a strict pollution law, Proposition 65, was approved in California by a large majority of Californians. The law aims to reduce threats to health from pesticides, toxic wastes, and other hazardous material.

The United Nations Environment Program (UNEP) was established in 1972 to "keep under review the world environmental situation in order to ensure that emerging environmental problems of wide international significance receive appropriate and adequate consideration by governments." Each year UNEP issues a report on the state of the world environment. It also has a databank on hazardous chemicals and working groups concerned with the transportation, handling, and disposal of hazardous wastes.

The European Community has introduced high standards of cleanliness for European beaches. Many fall below the standards, like this beach at Cherville, France.

Encouragement from Industry

Industries, too, are becoming more environmentally responsible as environmental issues hit the headlines.

One of the most well known industrial programs for reducing waste at its source is the Pollution Prevention Pays (3P) Principle introduced in 1975 by the U.S. 3M Corporation. The program looks for ways of saving money by reducing or reusing waste materials and it is supported by staff training and financial bonus plans.

The 3M Corporation found that the 3P Principle not only helped the environment, but also saved the company a lot of money in energy and running costs.

More recently, the multinational Dow Chemical Company launched its "Waste Reduction Always Pays" (WRAP) program to keep waste out of the environment. Dow says, "Waste reduction plays a crucial role in environmental protection and in the long-term growth of our business."

What You Can Do

"The global stage is set for positive environmental action, which has never been more needed." (UNEP)

It's your world that needs help, so what can you do? There are lots of simple practical ways you can help protect the environment. For example, look at what you throw away each day. How can you reduce the amount of things you throw away? What can be reused or recycled? Listed below are some suggestions that will help you to reduce waste and recycle it, wherever possible.

Many towns have recycling centers for waste paper, metal, and glass.

Reducing Waste

- *Don't accept an extra paper or plastic bag in stores if you're only going to throw it away.*

- *Write on both sides of paper; use recycled paper products when you can.*

- *Buy drinks in returnable bottles whenever possible.*

- *Avoid buying over-packaged goods.*

- *Are your eyes bigger than your belly? Don't take more food than you can eat!*

- *Save energy— switch off lights and heaters in rooms not being used; wear an extra sweater rather than turn up the heat.*

- *Use your legs—walk or bike when you can, rather than persuade someone to drive you.*

- *Don't drop litter.*

Reusing and Recycling

- *Clothes you no longer wear can be passed on or given to charity.*

- *Old toys, books, and games will be useful to someone else when you no longer want them, so don't throw them away.*

- *Waste paper—find out if there are any waste paper collections organized by your local government or charities.*

- *Cans—use an aluminum recycling center if you have one in your area but wash and squash the cans first.*

- *Bottles and glass—buy returnable bottles when you can; take used glass to the recycling center. If there is no recycling center in your area, write to the local government and ask for one.*

- *Make sure food waste goes onto the compost heap if you have one.*

Learning more

Find out what effect you, and those around you, have on the environment. Different people have different views on environmental issues—find out what they think about waste and recycling and why. There are lots of other books and magazines, as well as television and radio programs on the subject. Don't keep all this information to yourself—talk with other people!

Monitoring

Find out what happens to the waste in your house—where does it go? You can ask your local government. Watch for obvious signs of illegal waste dumping or polluted land, rivers, or air. If you think an individual or organization is behaving irresponsibly toward the environment, contact your local newspaper, government, or Department of Environmental Protection (DEP).

Support a campaign

There are many organizations campaigning for a cleaner, healthier environment and they need members to support them. They can also provide you with information and newsletters. A list of organizations is given on page 46.

You can help by learning more about environmental issues (above). Practical help is also needed, such as cleaning birds.

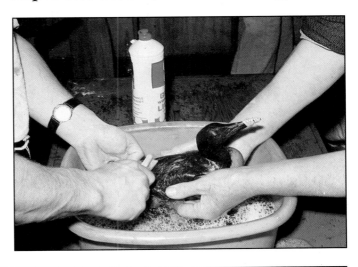

The Bellarmine Beasties

The Bellarmine Beasties is a club run at the Bellarmine Environmental Resource Center in Pollock, Scotland. In 1987, twenty-five members of the Beasties ran an environmental improvement project during their lunch hours, after school, and sometimes on the weekend, or on holidays.

They wanted to clean up the area around their schools, so they cleared litter from the playground, a footpath, and a local waterway. They also wanted the community to be more aware of litter and waste dumping in the area, so they promoted antilitter messages by producing posters, exhibitions, leaflets, and a video featuring an interview with a soda can!

The Beasties are enthusiastic about their project and they've won several national competitions for their hard work and ideas. Their message to the people of Pollock is "Keep your city in trim, dispose of litter properly in the bin."

43

Glossary

Acid Rain Rain, snow, mist, or hail that is made more acid by waste gases (sulfur dioxide and nitrogen oxide) discharged into the air.

Arable farming The farming of plant crops such as wheat, barley, and vegetables.

Atmosphere The layer of gases surrounding the Earth.

Biodegradable The term given to a substance that can be broken down by the natural processes of decomposition.

Conservation The protection and careful use of resources and the environment.

Decompose To break down dead material, putting nutrients back into the environment.

Element A simple substance composed of atoms.

Environment The surroundings of the world that humans and all other animals and plants live in.

Groundwater Water held in underground rocks and soil.

Habitat An area in which plants and animals live.

Humus Decomposed plant and animal material that is part of the soil.

Intensive farming Farming that uses high levels of machinery, equipment, and fertilizers to operate, usually in a small area of land. Livestock kept in these conditions are said to be "factory farmed."

Landfill site A place where solid waste is disposed of, usually a hole in the ground.

Marine pollution The pollution of the seas and oceans.

Microorganism A living animal or plant that is not visible to the naked eye.

Nutrients The materials that are necessary for growth and life, such as water, minerals, fats, and carbohydrates.

Organic waste Waste derived from animal or plant materials.

Pesticide A chemical used to kill plant pests such as aphids and slugs.

Pollution Damage caused to the environment by substances released into it. These substances are known as pollutants.

Radiation The emission, or giving out, of rays, particles, or waves by a substance.

Radioactive A radioactive substance is an element that breaks down into another element, at the same time giving out harmful radiation.

Reclamation Saving a waste product so that it can be reused.

Recycling The processing of waste products for reuse.

Refuse Something that is thrown away.

Resource Anything that is useful to living animals and plants.

Sewage The waste products and water from homes and from industry that are poured down the sink, drain, or toilets.

Smog A fog containing human-made pollutants.

Species A group of animals or plants that are capable of breeding with one another.

Toxic waste Waste products that are poisonous.

Unmonitored Without being checked by experts.

Urbanization The making of country areas into cities (urban areas).

Waste Something left over or not used.

Further Reading

Books

Miller, C. and Berry, L. *Waste* (Watts, 1986).
Pringle, L. *Throwing Things Away: From Middens to Resource Recovery* (Harper, 1986).

Showers, P. *Where Does the Garbage Go?* (Harper, 1974).
Weiss, M. *Toxic Waste: Cleanup or Coverup?* (Watts, 1984).

Pamphlets and Additional Materials

Aluminum can recycling pamphlets
Alcoa Aluminum Recycling
100 Clover Place
Edison, NJ 08818

CLASS Project: Conservation Learning Activities for Science and Social Studies. Ranger Rick: Recycling Reprints.
National Wildlife Federation
1412 16th St. NW
Washington, DC 20036

Comic book "Adventures of Ray Cycle."
Department of Environmental Protection
Solid Waste Management Unit
State Office Building
165 Capitol Avenue
Hartford, CT 06106

EPA Publication No. SW801: Let's Recycle! Lesson plans for grades K-6, 7-12.
U.S. Government Printing Office
Supt. of Documents
Washington, DC 20402

"Waste in Place" and other pamphlets and brochures.
Keep America Beautiful, Inc.
9 West Broad Street
Stamford, CT 06902

Periodic newsletter, library, and information service.
Centers for Plastics Recycling Research
Bldg. 3529
Busch Campus/Rutgers University
Piscataway, NJ 08855

Picture Acknowledgments

The publishers would like to thank the following for allowing their photographs to be reproduced in this book: Bruce Coleman 9 (NASA), 22 (Norman Myers), 23 (Norman Tomalin), 24 (Robert Carr), 34 below (Jeff Foott), 37 below; Frank Spooner Pictur (Stefano Nicozzi), 15 (Eric Bouvet), 20 (Gilbert Uzan), 32; Greenpeace 5, 19, 34 above; Hutchison Library 12 (Michael MacIntyre) (Lyn Gambles), 37 above; The Image Book 27 lower (© Fernando Buenu) Oxford Scientific Films 7 below (Jack Dermio), 8 (Rich Kulah) 22 center (Sean Morris), 25 above (Jack Dermio); (Photocredit 27 upper right (© Mary Kate Dunny); Photri *cover*, 7 above both, 30, 42; Rex Features 16, 17 below, 20, 21 above and below, 33 above and below, 35, 40; Royal Society for the Protectio Birds 43 (M. W. Richards); Topham Picture Library 17 above, 29 above and below, 31, 36 below, 39, 41; Wayland 25 left, 43 abov M. Wycherley 38, ZEFA 18, 36 above (Deuter). The artwork is by Stephen Wheele.

Useful Addresses

Children of the Green Earth
PO Box 95219
Seattle, Wash. 98145

Promotes and organizes children's tree planting projects and various educational activities. Publications.

Conservation Foundation
1250 24th Street N.W.
Washington, D.C. 20037

Promotes intelligent use of the earth's resources through research and communication. Publications, reports, and films.

Friends of the Earth
530 Seventh St., S.E.
Washington, D.C. 20003

An environmental pressure group that campaigns for conservation, environmental improvement, and a wise use of resources. Booklets and pamphlets are available.

Friends of the Earth Foundation
530 Seventh St., S.E.
Washington, D.C. 20003

Dedicated to education, research, litigation, and publishing for the preservation, restoration, and rational use of the earth's resources.

Greenpeace U.S.A.
1611 Connecticut Ave., N.W.
Washington, D.C. 20009

Initiates active measures to aid endangered species. Monitors conditions of environmental concerns including ocean dumping, acid rain, and test bannings on nuclear weapons.

Izaak Walton League of America
1401 Wilson Blvd., Level B
Arlington, Va. 22209

Works to educate the public on conserving, protecting, maintaining, and restoring the soil, forest, water, and other natural resources.

Sierra Club
730 Polk Street
San Francisco, Calif. 94109

Publishes a regular newsletter with details of environmental legislation in the United States.

World Nature Association
PO Box 673, Woodmoor Station
Silver Spring, Md. 20901

Naturalists—professional and amateur—interested in conservation and travel. Offers annual scholarship to an American educator in the natural sciences, grants for small research projects, conducts tours. Publications.

Index